T0131493

A *Daughter's* LOVE

DEANNA "MOORE" EDMONDSON

authorHOUSE®

AuthorHouse™
1663 Liberty Drive
Bloomington, IN 47403
www.authorhouse.com
Phone: 1 (800) 839-8640

Published by AuthorHouse   04/15/2020

ISBN: 978-1-7283-5899-4 (sc)
ISBN: 978-1-7283-5925-0 (e)

Print information available on the last page.

Introduction

This is the story of my love connection with my Mama.

Harriet Ann Moore
5-15-40   8-18-18

I have struggled with how I was gonna express my deep devotion for my Mama. This is my final chapter with my Mama. I have deep emotions and respect for a women I believe was born to become a "Mother".

She taught me everything I know about strength from with in.

She taught me what the meaning of unconditional love meant ♥

Remember me with smile's and laughter for that's how I will remember you all. If you can only remember me with tear's then don't remember me at all.

Laura Ingall's Wilder

This story is about her struggles and faith that would carry her all through her life.

My mother was born in 1940 a whopping 5 lbs. She was the third child and third daughter. She had older twin sisters. She grew up in hard times. Her parents divorcing when she was a small child. That would become a hardship on her as she adored her dad. But was only allowed to see him on Sunday's. Mama had a lot of medical emergency's but she also had a lot of blessings in her life. But she didn't know that until later in her life.

We also rejoice in our suffering's, because we know that suffering produces perseverance; perseverance, character; and character hope.

Romans 5:3-4

As a baby still in diaper's Mama had a medical emergency. As she was crawling on the floor my grandma noticed drop's of blood coming from Mama's diaper. Her rectum had fallen out of her. I don't know how that happens but it happened twice. The second time they sewed it back in her and told grandma if she were to have children, she couldn't have more then two. First blessing Mama had 6 yes that's right 6 children and God gave her a double blessing. He gave her 3 boy's 3 girl's, and it was boy, girl, boy, girl, boy, girl. She was meant for motherhood. But as a child she faced more challenges. At around 9 year's old Mama was sexual assaulted by a man who was doing an open house next to where she lived. Thank God he wasn't able to proceed with his plan's. As some one would show up to see the house up for sale. Mama so scared ran home. So afraid to say anything to her mother. Mama went deaf "psychosomatically" I can't imagine how she must of felt. And I don't understand how something like that happens. But Mama was deaf for a year. Another blessing she was sitting at the piano "grandma played" tapping at the key's when she screamed out I can hear! I can hear! Before Mama got her hearing back she learned to read lip's. I learned about that later in my life. What a blessing she can hear again but another double blessing not only can Mama hear she can now play the piano. She could not read music but if she heard a song she would tap on the piano key's and then she would be playing the song.

"Those who know Your name" will trust in You, for You Lord, have never forsaken those who seek You."

Psalm; 9:10

My Mama tried to teach me piano but because she didn't understand the key's she just knew she could play. It made it difficult for her. I now wish I would have learned on my own. That would have pleased her so much. My Mama was only close to one person in her young life her Grandma Ecko's because she wasn't allowed to see her daddy and her mother pushed her away because she adored her dad. Her grandma became her safe place. I think that's who taught my Mama about unconditional love. She would lose her daddy in 1959 finding out reading it in the newspaper. A year prior 1958 Mama's life would change. But as a child and teenager she had a lot of challenge's in her life that was preparing her for her greatest challenges and blessing's she married my father after only knowing him 3 months in June of 1958. Had her first child in 1959 and had a child every year until 1965.

She was born for motherhood. I was her second daughter and 4th child. My Mama's water broke a month before given birth to me. I can't imagine what that felt like for her. A dry birth. I was born a "blue baby" not breathing I think that's were my soul met my Mama's soul. I was born with mild cerebral palsy but Mama wouldn't learn of this until I was a small child. When I had a screaming pain in my leg. She took me to the doctor's and that's when she was told. Your daughter has mild CP on her right side. I think that's when Mama and I bonded in a different way. The guilt she carried with her she couldn't hide from me. My parent's didn't treat me any different but they were patient with me. My Mama was always so understanding with me. Although I was born not breathing. Once I did I became an instant cry baby, and I'm not ashamed of that. When it came to my Mama my emotion's were front and center.

As I grew up I became a rebellious teenager and that's when I learned of Mama being able to read lips. I learned you don't talk back to your Mama as loving as she was she was also spunky and you just knew when she meant business. As the year's went by I had my up's and down's with Mama, it wasn't until my adult life that I realized what a strong God fearing women she was. Because Mama did not attend church but she made sure we all went to Sunday school, and she was so proud of her baptism. She always talked about the man upstairs. For years I didn't know what that meant. Just like she would tell us she had a little birdy watching us. My Mama had a great sense of humor, but she had put the fear in me so I always tried to be a good girl. I was a Mama's girl the sensitive one I think that's why she was always so gentle with me.

She wasn't afraid to tell me when I was messing up. I had my moment's with Mama. But there was a silent understanding between us. And if there was any thing that ever had to do with her she had a hard time telling me that. Two things Mama didn't like to talk to me about my birth and her self. Remember I'm a cry baby when it come's to Mama. And over the year's I would be put through the test, as Mama faced so many medical challenges the strength and grace she showed really taught me about faith and purpose, I won't go in to details but Mama was faced with, gallbladder disease, heart disease with a triple bypass and later a pacemaker she called her buddy. Pancreases, bleeding in her belly twice, cardiac arrest, colon cancer, and her biggest challenge diabetes. But the one thing Mama always had on her side. Faith the man upstairs.

See when she had her gallbladder surgery she went into cardiac arrest so they had to stop and they placed a bag on her so the stones could pass in to. But they where also pumping posion off of her. I remember my dad saying to me. When you go in to see your mother you don't cry, oh ok dad because he knew. Well I walk into her room make eye contact and say I love you mommy and quickly exit her room, they had a tube down her mouth pumping the posion off, but the thing about Mama she just gave a thumb's up she never let on just how much pain she was in or how scared she was. I was witnessing true strength. It's at this time in my life I started begging for Mama's life. And continue for the next 38 years.

I realize now God was taken me and Mama on a spiritual journey. Through out my journey with all the medical issue's Mama faced I spent a lot of time on my knees.

Mama had several years were she managed her health. Her Dr. would tell her she was a great patient. Because she did her part as hard as it was for her. She gave up all the bad habit's in her life. She tried to eat healthy and exercise, if you were to know Mama you would never know she had any issue's because she just smiled her way through life. She was always more concerned with how you were doing then herself. When I learned of Mama's colon cancer I thought I was gonna die. My sister called me are you sitting down; I knew something was up. No just spit it out I said. Mom has colon cancer. Down on my knee's I went deep breath, trying not to cry I thought ok and hung up the phone. And then I lost it. Here I go begging dear God please I can't lose my mom she's my safe place. The one place I could go to and be me. Mama just had a present about her you just felt loved.

I knew if I needed a laugh I could go to Mama. She made me laugh so much. I really miss that. I will never have that again in this life. With Mama it was just so easy she was so real so true to her unconditional love. It just flowed out of her naturally I didn't have to say any thing when I was with Mama it was just a feeling she gave out. I was her darling she was my sunshine. It wasn't until her diabetes got the best of her that she started to show her pain. I think I have cried an ocean for Mama and I did it right in front of her. She would point her finger at me no! Crying I would look at her and say Mama I'm gonna cry forever. And then I would take a deep breath turn away from her feel the Man upstairs and look back at her and say ok Mama if your gonna be strong I will try. She would say that man up stair's listen's to me I would smile at her. Ok Mama. See Mama truly believed in her relationship with God. Like she knew the Heavenly Father personally. Faith is a beautiful thing. When she would have bad days she would say that man up stairs isn't listening to me. I will talk to him tonight. She kept her bible opened in her room her relationship with God was a private matter to her. The next day would come and I would speak with Mama. How are you feeling today Mama. I'm wonderful she said I had a talk with the man upstairs he listened to me he loves me she would say. He's good to me her faith was such a joy to see. She had me believing that. She would always bounce back because she went through so many medical challenges and the man upstairs always had her back.

"The Lord is my strength" and my shield; in him my heart trust, and I am helped; my heart exults, and with my song I give thanks to him. Psalm 28:7

2017 Started out to be a beautiful year not knowing it would be the beginning of the end. Oct 2017 Mama was on the phone face timing with my brother. See he bought her an Iphone so he could see her when he talked with her. They were talking and down Mama went to the ground my brother saw it and quickly hung up and called dad outside. Get in the house mom collapsed. Her heart stopped but her buddy kicked in and with all her strength Mama crawled to the back door where dad found her. Rushing her to the hospital. We her girl's she called us her posse rushed to her side, there she was sitting up smiling when can I go home. Mama slow down she always acted like she was ok she never wanted to show her fear. She looked at me even before I would cry she would say pointing her finger. No crying I would just sink inside Ok Mama but my soul was crying. Thinking how is Mama always so strong were does she get that strength. We all know "The man upstairs."

The love between a mother & daughter never end's.

"A son is a son until he take's a wife but a daughter is a daughter for life."

My connection was so deep that my Mama went home 16 year's to the day I was baptized.

8-18-18

The day I was born again was the same day the man upstairs took my Mama home.

2018 would become to worst year of my life. I would learn about strength and faith. I would feel the Holy Spirit I would witness God's glory. The journey begins my faith is being tested my love for my Mama is deepened as much as I feel like screaming as much as I feel like turning my back on the man up stair's I find myself becoming closer to God. Feeling lost the end is near but I didn't know that yet. So here we go. In April 2018 Mama would be hospitalized for 30 day's with a bacterial infection in her spine. "Osteomyelitis" how could this be happening to Mama. She spent all of April 2018 in the hospital. I really thought Mama was gonna beat this after all she came through so much she bounced back and she had her friend the man up stair's. But it turned out to be the biggest storm of her life. Mama loved life she loved her family her girls. Watching Mama go through the I.V. antibiotic treatment's were the hardest. I truly believe that is what brought her down. Because she was a heart patient and the kind of antibiotic they gave her sent her heart in to over drive. This is so hard its like reliving it all over. They were trying to kill an infection but at the same time they were destroying her heart her kidneys and sent her diabetes out of control. She never gave up being put on the C-Pap machine over and over night after night just trying to breathe. She would look up at us. I'm trying she would say, don't cry, I love you night after night. My birthday came Mama was still in hospital April 21st she sang Happy Birthday to me with the C-Pap machine on her face. I laid my head on her shoulder and cried, I love you Mama. And she felt so bad because she sang Happy Birthday to all her kid's and grand kids on there birthday it was a tradition we miss today.

Mama was finally able to come home from the hospital on her birthday May 15th she just told them I'm not spending my birthday in here. Mother's day was the day before and she tried so hard to come home, but she still had the I.V. hooked up. So we all came to her. So, Mama's home now and I'm thinking she's gonna be O.K. but because they used a sodium based antibiotic they enlarged her heart. And it was having trouble pumping the fluid off so Mama couldn't breathe from May 2018 to Aug 2018 she was rushed back and forth to the hospital, because her insurance wouldn't cover a C-Pap machine or oxygen for home care. Her last time August she was in hospital and they told her the heart med's aren't working anymore. The whole time Mama was in hospital she always made sure the nurse's smiled.

I thought to myself how does she do that. She's going through so much and she still smiling. I realized then she just loved life know matter how it came at her. She was my "Eye of the Tiger" she taught me so much about strength she just kept moving forward. She wasn't giving up but she was wearing a DNR the first time I seen it well you know. I cried like a baby. No!! Mama you're a fighter you're not giving up I was so angry I had to leave her room. I felt like how is that OK with everyone, it was Mama's choice. Oh no I'm not ready. Down on my knee's Father God please heal Mama I can't live without her. I'm not ready. My birthday in 2019 was to fall on Easter Sunday for the first time ever; I couldn't celebrate it with out Mama. She promised.

Hospice came in to her room and talk to her about going home. They would supply her with everything she needed at first she was like. I'm not ready to die; I'm saying that's right Mama she's fighting back. But then she thought about it and talked it over with dad. The next morning when I came to see her she told me she made her decision. It's burnt in my memory forever. "Deanna don't be mad at me but I'm going home on Hospice." Deep breath step back "uh ok" Mama whatever you want. I still had hope., "Faith" she started to get sick to her stomach her diabetes was out of control went way above 1600 she was sweating she had this little fan one of the nurse's had bought her prior to this trip to hospital. My daughter stayed with her grandma and I ran to my car drove to her house grab her

24

fan raced back to the hospital they had called for a special team to come and push insulin in to her. I now know the man up stairs removed me from that horrific scene. My Mama wasn't the same after that. I was so angry so out of my mind but trying to hold it together for her. They stabilized her and she went home. Aug 14th 2018 my sister's and niece's and daughter stayed with Mama. Those last 4 day's taught me a lot about faith and true love. Let the journey began I didn't stay the first night I was just to angry. My sister called me that night. Will you please come. I came, hospice was already there the night before so she had her oxygen. She was on the oxygen for 2 nights but my love and devotion came all in one night, Mama never knew how to tell me anything bad when it came to her she always tip toed around it. She didn't know how to tell me she wasn't gonna be here for my Easter birthday. She said to my sister how do I tell her. Her reply your just gonna have to say it mom. So my sister had me step out on the front porch looked right at me. Your gonna have to tell mom it's ok she's not gonna be here for your birthday, deep inside I thought no way I'm not giving up on Mama. But I stepped back in Mama's room she sat on the side of her bed with her eye's close's rocking put her hand's up straight at me, eye's still closed "Why can't you let me go." in a firm voice. I was so taken back by that I felt like God put His hand over my mouth, I took a step back and said it's between you and God Mama. Why did I say that I should be on my knee's crying my eyes out. So she put her hands in the air. Eye's closed looked up and said "Take me

I'm ready." I felt my soul and Mama's soul separate. My heart would forever skip a beat I felt a strength come over me. She couldn't make it in to see her cardiologist and she had a long beautiful friendship with him. He faced time her. At this point Mama was laying in her bed no oxygen required. She kept her eye's closed she asked him straight forward. Am I dying. He said unfortunately yes you are my dear, he told her he loved her and she was a pleasure to know. She said Ok and laid her head down and waited for the med tech to come turn off her pace maker. Her little buddy did his job for her for many year's. I didn't cry I felt at that moment the man up stair's pushed me back.

That night the family came and spent time with her. Hugging her, holding her hand. I would just peak around the corner look at her and say I love you and walk away. At this point I think I looked like I was walking around numb.

Friday night came and Mama was breathing peacefully on her own, the first time in 5 month's we all noticed Mama was glowing. She (her legs) was becoming youthful. Everyone notice her legs they were beautiful not a scar nothing. What were we witnessing. Mama laid quietly but for 3 day's. We heard Mama sit up, eye's closed help help we would go running, but for the longest time she would lay so quietly, Bible opened on her dresser she had a light up pen laying in her Bible. Sitting at the dining room table evening time it was dark we saw something blinking in Mama's room it was her pen it just started blinking different color's my niece went in grabbed the pen and tried to turn it off. But it wouldn't go off it just kept blinking. I asked my niece at that point go check grandma's oxygen. So she went in put the oximeter machine on her finger it was 48 percent. And then I knew it has begun. Don't panic, don't cry. So we just sat and waited. My sister would go check on her. Mama was soaked and wet. Her kidney's have just failed her I thought to myself. They went in cleaned Mama up and she just laid there so peaceful. Trying to stay calm we continued to sit and wait. I don't think anyone got any sleep taking turn's up and down for 4 days. Saturday morning come's it's early and we here, water, we all jump up oh my it's Mama. My niece run's in, my daughter goes for water I get up and pace back and forth. The most spiritual and peaceful moment is about to happen. The man upstairs is here. I didn't feel the need to go to my knee's I didn't feel the need to beg for her life.

I just sat down in her big blue chair, month's earlier I have given my Mama a glass rose. She had it sitting on her table were she would sit. Some thing came over me the Holy Spirit. I got up grabbed a news paper wrapped the glass rose in it went out side put it on the ground and stomped on it. I came back in told my daughter get the Bible open it to Psalm 23 lay it next to her, hurry I couldn't go in there something was stopping me. I felt her leaving but I was so numb I wasn't in control, why wasn't I with her, I thought

I didn't want to leave this way, the rest of my thought's are all a blur. My dad left to go get Mama ice I went back out side pacing back and fourth. Praying deep breathing. I came back in my niece walked out of her room with her head down, is she gone she just quietly said yes with her head down, sister went to check yes she's gone. All I remember is I screamed so loud saying ok Mama is sleeping shh Mama is sleeping all the breath left my body at this point. I couldn't breathe gasping for air and saying over and over Mama's sleeping don't bother Mama. My younger sister went in to full panic her daughter had to cover her mom's body with hers because she just wanted to run screaming as I'm gasping for air my niece trying to calm me down my daughter slid down the wall with complete silence. Dad still gone not knowing Mama went home to the man up stairs. But it was beautiful for Mama. She had a drink of water looking at my niece said "I love you", "We are all here grandma." She laid her head down and quietly went home, eyes closes she just looked like she was sleeping.

I never went back in her room I didn't witness any of this but I felt it. So many months of struggling to breath Mama had no struggles when she passed away. The man up stairs has carried Mama through out her life and was right there to take her home. At the same time was right there holding my hand keeping me at a distances. See I don't think Mama could have had this beautiful journey if she thought I was right there needing her. Mama you are the best I adore you my best friend. The unconditional love this human being showed me was something I know I will never have again in my life. I could be myself I could laugh, cry, get mad and her love stayed the same.

Mama and I didn't see eye to eye all the time we had are moment's but the one thing I knew deep inside is Mama was always on my team she loved me she always had my back. I remember sitting in her hospital room I looked at her and said I'm sorry Mama for ever causing you any hardship she looked at me and said don't you say that. There's nothing to forgive. I love you my darling. I can't express what that did for me. Her love was just so easy so simple. Mama went through a lot in her life it's never been a easy life but she loved life so much and you just knew it. She smiled her way through it all. There was nothing life could throw at her that she didn't bounce back from.

If I was taught anything from her it was to smile, the man up stairs will take care of it. It's not something she said but how she lived her life. This is my story my way to remember my Mama. Strength, love and the man up stair's is all she needed and passed on to me. Thank you Mama.

I love you to the moon and back.

Final Thoughts

As I write this I think to myself how did Mama go through so much in here life and not be bitter or angry at the world. I think being a mother brought her so much joy. To be able to give all that love she had in her that she didn't get to show growing up just shined right through as soon as she became a Mama. Mama was just human like anyone else but to us she was are hero. She loved life know matter what and that's what she taught us. Smile life is just so beautiful.

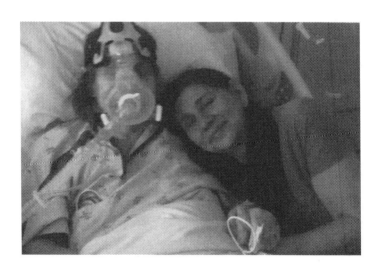

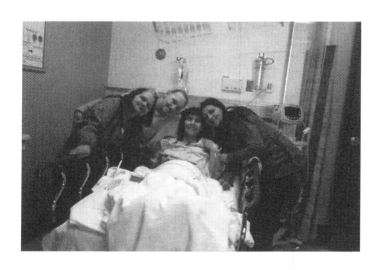

True love
60 years

2017
Love of her life
Mama and Dad

I started this book in 2016 but had to set it aside due to Mama's illness and my own issue's with my vision. I became blind in my left eye, the ending of my book is not what I wanted with deep sadness Mama passed away before I could finish. But I have since had eye surgery and through my blurry vision with God guiding my hand this book will come to life. Mama's message to the world.

Love one another and remember to smile.

We also rejoice in our sufferings, because we know that suffering produces perseverance; perseverance, character, and character,

Hope

Romans 5:3-4

Dedications

My Mama's love was felt deep in my soul, my heart will forever skip a beat for her. I know Mama is at peace I'm grateful that she rest now she's home with the man up stair's but I now have to live with half a soul until we are together again. She gave me strength and faith and that's what I will walk with. How do you repay someone who gave so much, 6 children and we all have our own story our own love story. As I write this with my eyes full of tear's I find myself in my doorway looking at the moon. Mama that's how I connect to her. How do you connect to your Mama, a scent a song the morning sun. Here is a poem and the Eulogy my brother wrote. I think I don't need to say anymore.

Mom, Thank you for being you. You were the best a kid could hope for. You made us all feel special! Your loyalty to dad has been unreal in modern times. You've inspired us to be better people, now more than ever! Mom we'll always miss you and think about you, you are a beacon in our hearts to help those in need

You cared about everybody and for that we thank you,

Our friends all called you mom, because you were a natural,

You were the ultimate momma bear, we felt safe with you, we felt loved if there's a heaven above us then your surly there.

Reminiscing with your mom dad and sisters, that brings happiness to our hearts just thinking about it. You bring happiness to our hearts. Sure it starts out as sadness, but soon turns into happiness, just thinking about you, how awesome you were as a parent, you were more then a parent you were a friend. Mom. I could ramble on all night about how beautiful you are, but really. There's no need for words. They don't really apply when speaking of you, your a superhero and you'll live on in our hearts.

If roses grow in Heaven, Lord
please pick a bunch for me,
Place them in my Mother's arms
and tell her they're from me.
Tell her I love her and miss her,
and when she turns to smile,
Place a kiss upon her cheek
and hold her for awhile.
Because remembering
her is easy,
I do it every day,
But there's an ache
within my heart
That will never go away.

Rest now Mama you earned it. Shhh Mama's

Sleeping xoxo

PSALM 23

"The LORD is my shepherd I
shall not want. He makes me lie
down in green pastures; He leads
me beside the still waters. He
restores my soul; He leads me in
the paths of righteousness for His name's sake
name's sake. Yea, though I walk through
the valley of the shadow of
death, I will fear no evil; For You
are with me; Your rod and Your
staff, they comfort me. You prepare
a table before me in the presence of
my enemies; You anoint my head
with oil; My cup runs over. Surely
goodness and mercy shall follow
me All the days of my life; And I
will dwell in the house of the
LORD Forever."

Thank you to Marsha, Rebecca, Trisha, Judith, Stephanie and sisters, Regina Little Carol Ruiz. For your time and support in the writing and dedication of this book.

Printed in the United States
By Bookmasters